The Phony Litvinenko Murder

Finally the truth after 5 years: The story
told by the media doesn't match the facts.

By William Dunkerley

ⓟ Omnicom Press

Published by
Omnicom Press
New Britain, CT, USA
Publishers since 1981

www.OmnicomPress.com

Library of Congress Control Number: 2011919082
ISBN-10 0615559018
ISBN-13 978-0615559018
Printed in the United States of America

This book is dedicated to the Litvinenko family. May they achieve success in their search for the truth and discover peace therein.

Preface

In 2007 I was commissioned by the organizers of the World Congress of the International Federation of Journalists to study the media coverage of the Litvinenko poisoning. The Congress was held in Moscow, where I presented my report. Now, five years after the poisoning, this book serves both to reflect upon and update my findings.

Litvinenko quickly became a household name across the globe. Stories about him led news broadcasts and made worldwide headlines. For example:

"Russian Ex-Agent 'Poisoning' Probed"

"Poisoning Prevented Litvinenko from Disclosing Names of Politkovskaya's Killers"

"British Police Investigate Poisoning of Putin

Critic"

I've studied the stories that followed these headlines, along with many other reports, both Western and Russian, to put everything into context for you, i.e., a description of the essence of the story, with a focus on its beginnings. Then, I've gone on to analyze the press coverage of the story and present my findings. And finally, I've similarly examined media coverage in the fall of 2011, to bring things up to date on the 5th anniversary of the poisoning and death of Litvinenko.

What you'll read here is a story and media reportage full of contradictions, claims and counterclaims, twists and turns, and unexpected relationships. I found that:

—many headlines and storylines in this case have no apparent basis in fact

—one of the major themes in coverage doesn't even make sense

—Alexander Litvinenko changed his theory of who poisoned him, but the press gave that little attention

—a web of mysterious connections went

largely uncommented upon in the press

—there was an active PR push behind the Litvinenko story by parties interested in spinning it

—the biased coverage of Litvinenko fits into a larger ideological approach in Western reporting on today's Russia.

The focus of this book is on the media coverage of the story. It is not intended as an investigative piece into the circumstances of Litvinenko's death.

W.D.
November 2011

Contents

Chapters

Chapter 1

A Phony Murder?

The media covered a fantasy, but missed the real story.

LONDON, November 2006: The phony Litvinenko murder story begins in the weeks leading to the gruesome death of Alexander Litvinenko. He was a newly-minted British citizen who had emigrated from Russia just six years earlier. Litvinenko succumbed to poisoning, apparently by radioactive polonium-210.

Some say in Soviet times Litvinenko had been a KGB spy. Others claim he simply was a spy-agency prison guard who got fired, later to return to the Russian security service in a job investigating organized crime. It is difficult to sort out where the truth lies in all that.

Just before moving to London, Litvinenko had become caught up in a series of murky criminal charges against him. For a time he was imprisoned. But, during a break, when he had been released on his own recognizance, and despite written assurances that he remain in Russia, he fled.

Stories have it that he went to Ukraine on a forged passport, then to Turkey where he requested asylum in the United States. Like an entangled Russian novel, the story goes on to say that the U.S. turned thumbs down on his request. Luckily, Alexander Goldfarb was on hand. He's an associate of Boris Berezovsky, the former Russian business tycoon. Berezovsky, who also fled to London to avoid prosecution, has since been convicted in-absentia of crime back in Russia. (Are you following all this?) Goldfarb helped Litvinenko get on an Istanbul to Moscow flight that happened to go via London. On the ground in London for a transit stop, Litvinenko made a successful request for asylum.

Is any of that true? I don't know. Like much about the Litvinenko matter, it is hard to separate fact from fiction. And there are a lot of things that just don't make sense.

An Oracle from Nowhere

Few people had ever heard of Litvinenko in his pre-London days. He was little known in Russia and in the world. Indeed, he was practically obscure. But that all changed when he landed in London. All of a sudden,

Litvinenko became a newsmaker of international proportion.

He lit into Russian president Vladimir Putin with a series of inflammatory accusations. Litvinenko accused Putin of:

—bombing Russian apartment buildings
—being involved in organized crime
—killing journalist Anna Politkovskaya
—being a pedophile

While not naming Putin specifically, Litvinenko also alleged that the violent 2002 Moscow theater siege and the tragic 2004 siege in Beslan may have been carried out on orders of the FSB, the successor agency to the KGB.

Ultimately, of course, Litvinenko reportedly accused Putin of being responsible for his poisoning.

Making Sense of Nonsense

There is one gnawing question about all this, however. It's not about the accusations, but about Litvinenko. Why did the world care about what this unknown person had to say about all these controversies and tragedies?

From what I could see, he wasn't offering any startling evidence for his accusations. What he gave to the media are claims, apparently unsubstantiated claims. The world is full of unnoticed, unsubstantiated claims about this or that, made by people we've never heard of.

Why were Litvinenko's claims treated so differently? In particular, where were the facts behind the accusation that Litvinenko was poisoned on orders from Putin? The "Putin did it" theme was perhaps the most explosive part of the media coverage of the Litvinenko poisoning. But, where were the facts? Once again, the claims seem to have been more prominent than the facts. What a failure that was of international journalism.

Something Important Was Missing

Now jump from 2006 to 2011.

A new flurry of news stories emerges. The theme is similar. Headlines trumpet a renewed investigation into the culpability of the Russian state in the murder of Litvinenko.

As I looked over those stories, I came to

wonder: now after five years, what had the London coroner found on the matter? But as I searched for the answer, I couldn't find anywhere that the coroner had even concluded that Litvinenko was a victim of homicide. So, I asked the coroner if my suspicion was correct, that there was no finding of homicide or as to the cause of death. The response came that there was not.

An official conclusion on the manner of death — homicide, suicide, accident, natural causes, undetermined — was never reached.

Whether or not the coroner has yet classified the death may not prove anything one way or another about the nature of the death itself. But it certainly does reflect directly upon the nature of the journalism related to the case. And something seems fishy there.

All along, media outlets had been reporting this as an unqualified murder. But it wasn't. It was merely an alleged murder. The coroner had yet to make a determination. The Litvinenko story isn't what it seemed to be on the surface.

And that's what *The Phony Litvinenko Murder* is all about: media claims that Putin or the Russian state had been behind the death of Litvinenko.

One thing that keeps striking me is that the facts to back up the most remarkable claims seem to be missing. What's more, the coroner has yet to decide that there was in fact a murder. It seems like the news media just made up the whole story or accepted claims without validating them.

A Clearer Perspective

In this book you'll see how the Litvinenko news coverage contains explanations that inexplicably morph from one version into another, that some renditions simply don't make sense — and that amid all this there remains the nagging question of how this unknown person with seemingly outlandish accusations and few facts became the news star that he did.

Someone suggested that I should have named this book "Alex in Wondergrad." Like *Alice in Wonderland*, the Litvinenko story is full of nonsensical elements that defy logical reasoning. The fact-lacking stories seem almost like they have a trickster behind them. If one tries to follow the trail of purported facts, things just seem to become curiouser and curiouser.

What's the Story?

When journalists go out on an assignment, one of the first things they ask themselves is "what's the story here"? In other words, what is the most newsworthy angle. Then they look for what is reliably true and report on it.

Indeed, what's the story here? Is it the unverified rantings of an unknown and disaffected person who some say held a big-time grudge? That's not the real story here. And besides, who knows if any of that is even true!

But what about the tale of how those rantings became a top story around the world? Now, that's something. That's the story here. The story is the story.

But no one covered it.

Chapter 2
How Big Was the Story?

There's a message in the size. But what is it?

BEGINNING in late November 2006, this was one of the largest news stories in the world. The allegation that Litvinenko was murdered on orders of Russian president Vladimir Putin was explosive.

Just how big was the story? In March 2007, to approximate the story's magnitude, and to put it into some perspective, I did several comparative investigations on Russian- and English-language search engines. I examined not only stories in the mass media, but also references in blogs, on websites, and in media archives.

In English, "+Litvinenko" combined with "+Murder" brought 585,000 entries on Google. The same search with "Politkovskaya" instead of Litvinenko produced 221,000 hits. Anna Politkovskaya was the crusading journalist who was murdered in Moscow just a month prior to the poisoning of Litvinenko. I followed the Politkovskaya search then with "Klcbnikov," the name of the American of Russian descent who was the founding editor of *Forbes* magazine in Russia. He was murdered in Moscow in July, 2004. That search yielded 53,600 hits.

This put the Litvinenko topic well above the others. Of course, it's hard to tell exactly what factors went into those differing rankings. Klebnikov had been murdered over two years earlier. Some of the Web pages about him may have been removed over time. But, Politkovskaya's murder was recent. It is puzzling why there is such a disparity between her and Litvinenko's search results. Was it because the British press just went hog wild over the story?

As to coverage in Russia, one journalist claims that there has been indifference. Tony Halpin, Moscow correspondent for the London *Times* wrote: "The fate of Alexander Litvinenko may be hot news in Britain, but Russia's press is almost completely ignoring him." He cites a page-one story in the English-language *Moscow Times* as an exception. Otherwise, "none of the major dailies covers the story today (November 21)," he asserts.

But, that was not all that journalist Halpin

asserted. He went on to say:

"...the papers simply don't believe their readers will be interested." What was his source for that insight? None was given.

"Russians may be divided over whether the FSB had a hand in poisoning Mr. Litvinenko..." Source? None cited.

"...but they are almost certainly united in not wanting to read about it." Source? None cited.

"They are quite willing to believe that the Russian state is capable of such actions..." Source? None cited.

Halpin's allegations may or may not be true. However, his readers would have no way of judging that. He offered no facts, just a viewpoint that he failed to substantiate. That leaves one wondering whether any of what he wrote about portrays an accurate picture.

I looked further into Halpin's premise that the Litvinenko story was being ignored in Russia. Before Halpin's story appeared, his paper, the *Times*, had covered the Litvincnko case on two previous days, the 19th and

20th. In the U.S., the *New York Times*, the *Washington Post*, and the *Los Angeles Times* didn't begin coverage until the 20th. But, in Russia, several online news outlets kicked off coverage on November 11, as did a Chechen website apparently located outside of Russia. That same day, the Russian Service of BBC broadcast an interview with Litvinenko himself. By the 13th, three Moscow papers (*Kommersant*, *Moscow Times*, and *Moscow News*) had picked up the story. But, the earliest story I found in the London *Times* wasn't until the one on November 19.

The London *Times* may have been late, but it made up for it with the number of stories. I counted six Litvinenko stories on the 20th and six on the 21st. With the one story on the 19th, that's a total of 13 stories in three days. During that time, the *New York Times* ran just one story. The *Washington Post* ran three, but one was an editorial.

So, the level of Russian coverage around the time of Halpin's story was actually consistent with that in the American press during the same period. Moreover, coverage in Russia began a full eight days earlier than it did in the *Times*.

Isn't it strange that Halpin's stories were so off base?

A search engine investigation also refuted Halpin's claim that the story found no interest in Russia. The same searches I described earlier were repeated in Russian on Rambler, the Russian search engine. That yielded more hits for "Litvinenko" than the Google search: 690,000. But, this time, the disparity with "Politkovskaya" was far less. The Politkovskaya search produced 578,048 hits. Klebnikov, 41,455.

That left the nagging question of, when compared to Politkovskaya, why was the Litvinenko story so much larger in the English-language searches? The poisoning happened in the UK, of course. But was that the only reason? On the surface, the exaggerated and late-coming interest in the Litvinenko case in English language media seems to defy reasonable explanation. It is very curious.

(Note: All the search engine investigations referenced above were done in March 2007. Searches done at other times will produce variously differing results.)

Chapter 3
The Story's Timeline

How the story unfolded...

IT appears that the Litvinenko story first broke at 8:35 AM Moscow Time on November 11, 2006, in a report on KavkazCenter.com, a Chechen news site. It carried the headline "FSB Attempted to Murder Russian Defector in London."

Later in the day, the story was picked up by the Regnum News Agency. Utro.ru had it, too. They reported getting it from a Chechen source. Lenta.ru carried the story, and referred to an Echo Moskvy story of the same day, which in turn had referenced Chechen media.

The BBC Russian Service ran a telephone interview with Litvinenko at 4:48 PM. They told me it had been taped in London about an hour earlier.

On November 13, three more Moscow outlets had stories that referred to Litvinenko: *Kommersant* ran the headline, "Litvinenko Did Not Digest the Information," and explained that Litvinenko said he was "poisoned when meeting an informer who delivered documents about the murder of Russian journalist Anna Politkovskaya." The *Moscow Times* reported that Litvinenko claimed he "might have been poisoned by a man who had sought to meet him, saying he had documents related to the death of the journalist." Later *Moscow News* carried the same information with attribution to the *Moscow Times*.

What's significant about these reports is that they indicate Litvinenko originally believed he had been poisoned by the person who had given him documents about Politkovskaya's death. That fits the description given of Italian Mario Scaramella in other stories. Litvinenko was not blaming Russian President Vladimir Putin.

Yuri Felshtinsky backed that up. He is the person who coauthored with Litvinenko a book that accused Putin of blowing up apartment buildings in Russia. In a December 5 episode of *The Charlie Rose Show* on the American Public Broadcasting System, Felshtinsky said, "He done it in conversation with me, we were talking this probably fifteen or twenty minutes by phone probably on 8th November, and at that time

Litvinenko was sure that this was Mario Scaramella who poisoned him."

Felshtinsky also indicated that before he died, Litvinenko came to say that Putin was involved. What happened between these early reports and the statement of November 21, in which Litvinenko accused Putin? For one thing, Boris Berezovsky paid him a hospital visit on Friday, November 17, according to the *Washington Post*. After that meeting, Berezovsky said Litvinenko had told him there was no doubt he had been poisoned by an "order from President Putin to kill him."

That should have left journalists wondering why Litvinenko changed his story. Had he made up his own mind based on new information, or was he influenced by others? I don't know.

There is little doubt, however, that within two days after Berezovsky's hospital visit, the media blitz commenced, and the world came to know about Alexander Litvinenko like never before.

Following Litvinenko's death on November 23, investigators began following the radioactive trail of polonium and focused in on the involvement of two Russians, Dmitry Kovtun and Andrei Lugovoi. On May 22, 2007, Lugovoi was charged with the murder of Litvinenko.

Revising History

There's an old joke from Soviet times about revisionist history that went something like this: In the West the news is always changing, but history stays the same, but in the Soviet Union it's always the same old news, but history changes.

In mid 2007 there was a revision in the story about who Litvinenko initially believed poisoned him. According to the reports cited above it was Scaramella. But on June 10, 2007, the *Washington Post* reported, "Immediately after Litvinenko began feeling ill Nov. 1, she [Litvinenko's wife] recalled, he told her that he suspected Lugovoi of poisoning him with the tea."

As you'll see in a later chapter, there was an earlier switcheroo in the account of who wrote Litvinenko's deathbed "Putin did it" accusation.

It appears that in the fantasyland of the Litvinenko story, history is malleable.

Chapter 4
The Spy Who Knew Too Much

Was he murdered to keep him from talking?

MANY news reports connected the Litvinenko poisoning with his interest in the Anna Politkovskaya murder. The French news agency AFP reported on November 19, that he "fell ill after meeting a contact at a London sushi bar who purportedly had information on the murder of Russian journalist Anna Politkovskaya."

On November 20, the *Washington Post* put it this way: "British police are investigating the poisoning of a former Russian spy and outspoken critic of President Vladimir Putin," adding that he became ill after lunching with "a man who gave him documents related to the recent killing of Anna Politkovskaya."

The *New York Times*, also on November 20, pointed out that "Russian authorities had no immediate comment on suggestions in news reports that the Russian secret service had poisoned Mr. Litvinenko, who is hospitalized and seriously ill, because he had criticized former colleagues and President Vladimir V.

Putin."

Perhaps *Izvestia* expressed this theme most succinctly in a November 13 headline that read, "Poisoning Prevented Litvinenko from Disclosing Names of Politkovskaya's Killers." It went on to report that "he met with Italian Mario Scaramella, who had promised to send him important information on the murder of journalist Anna Politkovskaya."

A timeline of the Litvinenko poisoning that was presented in the *Guardian* on November 20, even indicates that the Politkovskaya murder was at the start of it all.

On that same day the *Independent* reported, "Sources close to Mr. Litvinenko said he believed the Russian Federal Security Bureau (FSB), the successor to the KGB, poisoned him to stop four agents being named as suspects in the murder of the journalist Anna Politkovskaya — who investigated human rights abuses in Chechnya."

Unanswered Questions

This "spy-who-knew-too-much" theme really took off across the world. But, it left two very significant questions unanswered. The first is, why was Alexander Litvinenko investigating the Politkovskaya murder? He was not identified as a journalist. No one claimed that he was a private investigator working on behalf of a client. Why was he doing this? And, might the answer to that shed some light upon the circumstances of his poisoning?

But, it seems no journalists were asking these questions.

The second significant question has to do with the underlying premise, i.e., that he knew something that would be incriminating of others, and that he was poisoned to keep him from talking.

Didn't time prove that to be false?

In the three weeks before his death, Litvinenko didn't reveal these secrets. He gave a number of interviews, but didn't name names and didn't spill the beans.

That raises one very big challenge to the plausibility of this storyline. The spy-who-knew-too-much theme just didn't add up. Yet, I didn't find where any journalists came to grips with that. It is as if everyone pretended that this story angle made sense. In reality, however, there was no apparent sense to it. It's just another unexplained, illogical peculiarity relating to the Litvinenko case.

And in the end, adding to the fantasy-world quality of the Litvinenko story, the "spy-who-knew-too-much" theme just seemed to fade out of view, with the coverage morphing into yet other nonsensical themes.

Chapter 5
The Thorn in the Side

Was he killed because he was an irritant?

EVEN larger than the spy-who-knew-too-much myth is the "thorn-in-the-side" theme. The idea behind it is that Litvinenko had been mouthing off too much with scandalous allegations against Putin and the FSB, the Russian security service. That presumably was the motive for the alleged murder of Litvinenko. It was to shut him up. That concept is the premise for the "Putin did it scenario."

This theme was expressed with great clarity in a *Guardian* story. It quoted Boris Berezovsky saying, "Vladimir Putin authorized the murder of Alexander Litvinenko." No evidence was offered, however. You'd think that even a novice journalist would have known to ask Berezovsky for some supporting facts.

The *Sunday Times* (London) reported that Litvinenko himself said he believed he had been attacked to avenge his defection. But again, no facts.

Nonetheless, on November 20, the *Guardian* ran the headline, "Former KGB officer was poisoned because he was enemy of Putin, say friends." No facts back that up. It is attributed with the vague reference of "friends." But with such flimsy evidence, how is it that this allegation rose to the level of headline material? It doesn't make sense that a responsible journalist would give that aspersion such a big play.

Gilding the Lily

The "thorn-in-the-side" theme was frequently embellished by the way in which Litvinenko was described. He was variously referred to as a Putin critic, a former Russian spy and outspoken critic of Putin, a KGB agent turned dissident, and a former KGB operative who became a prominent dissident opposed to Russian President Vladimir Putin. These terms and phrases are all consistent with the "thorn-in-the-side" imagery.

On the other hand, Litvinenko also could legitimately have been referred to as an author, a journalist, a defector, a traitor, an outlaw, or as someone who fled justice. However, these characterizations, while having ostensibly as much connection to reality as the former, don't support the same imagery. These terms were almost never seen in news reports.

Russian Assassins Loose in London?

The London *Times* reported on November 23, 2006, "Russia's repeated denials that it was involved in the poisoning of Alexander Litvinenko has done little to ease concerns that the Kremlin remains ready to use force abroad against its enemies. This year the Duma, the lower house of the Russian parliament, passed laws allowing the Russian head of state to use special units to eliminate individuals regarded as a threat to Russian security wherever they are found."

That certainly is a speculation-provoking law. But, neither the *Times* nor any other news outlet seemed to have any evidence that the referenced law had been invoked. The venerable *Times* seems to be resorting to innuendo. But for what reason? Isn't this really strange?

This foreign assassin aspect of the story saw world news outlets dueling with one another. On November 20, the London *Times* had written, "Britain will be plunged into its worst crisis with Russia since President Putin came to power if a Scotland Yard investigation into the poisoning of a former Russian security agent leads back to the Kremlin, diplomats said last night."

The next day, in response, *Pravda*, accused the *Times* of speculation, indicating that Russia has had good relations with Great Britain throughout the tenure of Tony Blair. Then, the *Times* came back with a story entitled, "Kremlin's denials fall flat," elaborating upon concerns "that the Kremlin remains ready to use force abroad against its enemies."

It is certainly understandable that any country would be concerned about the possibility of foreign agents killing targets within its sovereign territory. It was just in February 2004, that the former Chechen leader, Zelimkhan Yanderbiyev had been killed in Qatar. When a court in Doha found two men guilty of the crime, the trial judge said "the men had been acting on orders from the Russian leadership," according to BBC.

Is the idea of violating sovereignty in order

to kill someone really something that can account for the uproar over Litvinenko?

Well, remember, the Litvinenko murder produced 585,000 Google hits. The Yanderbiyev assassination: 886. So much for that explanation.

But why did this theme lead to so many headlines in the Litvinenko case? Indeed, were there any facts to substantiate the "Putin did it" scenario?

Police Have a Suspect

In May 2007, a Russian named Andrei Lugovoi was charged by British officials with the murder of Litvinenko. A May 23 *New York Times* headline read, "Russian Is Accused of Poisoning Ex-KGB Agent." Lugovoi is described in the lead simply as a Russian businessman. The *Times* describes Litvinenko himself as a "foe of the Kremlin," an "anti-Putin crusader," and a "whistleblower." Noteworthy is that both Lugovoi and Litvinenko are described as working for Berezovsky during the 1990s.

The *Times* article adds, "The hand of those around Vladimir Putin was clearly visible in the murder," quoting Yuri Felshtinsky, described also as an associate of Boris Berezovsky.

So, let's see, the crux of the *Times* story is that close associates of Putin picked Lugovoi, a man who had been closely associated with Putin arch-enemy Berezovsky, to assassinate Litvinenko in London. I don't know if any of that is true. But, let's assume for a moment that it is. Why didn't the *Times* at least remark upon the incongruity of picking and trusting someone associated with Putin's enemies to pull off a volatile, covert, murderous mission? This was like reporting a story in which 2 plus 2 is said to equal 3 — and then failing to question that computational inconsistency.

The whole Litvinenko case is certainly a big mystery. But the illogical, nonsensical, and fantastical way it has been covered by otherwise respected media organizations is without question the mystery's mystery.

Chapter 6
The Media's Dirty Little Secret

Uh oh, the secret's out now.

SO we've seen that the media story about Litvinenko was inexplicably large, that the major themes of reporting seem quite fantastical, and that much of the reportage appears to be very one-sided.

What could possibly account for these strange circumstances?

There is a strong clue in some of the 2006 media coverage of Litvinenko. The *Financial Times* reported that Lord Bell, who "promoted Margaret Thatcher towards Downing Street in 1979, was cooperative in answering media inquiries" regarding Litvinenko. The *Independent* said Bell's company, Bell Pottinger Communications, "handled media calls about Mr. Litvinenko and arranged for the distribution of photographs taken of him in hospital." The *Financial Times* also added that "Lord Bell has been representing Boris Berezovsky for four years." Berezovsky is, of course, the Russian-born billionaire frequently tied to Litvinenko in media reports. He lives in

Great Britain, where he was granted political asylum.

These descriptions add up to something that's called a "managed story." It is quite a common phenomenon. Basically, this method is used when someone or some organization wants to see a particular story propagated in the mass media. Typically, it will involve a press release, usually written in a way that makes it easy for news outlets to simply lift copy and use it. It can be accompanied with photographs and video. Often the agent who is managing the story will arrange interviews between media staff and prominent or key people who are associated with the story.

Have you ever seen similar stories that appear in the coverage of multiple news outlets? Perhaps it was an item about Earth Day, or Breast Cancer Awareness Month, or other charitable or public awareness activities. This kind of coverage is typically a result of the managed story approach.

Politicians use the same methodology. When you see a political newsmaker making the rounds on various political news and commentary TV programs, it is probably an example of a managed story.

Evidence from Academia

Dr. Felicitas Macgilchrist, a researcher at the Georg Eckert Institute in Braunschweig, Germany, wrote about this in her book *Journalism and the Political*. Indeed, she devoted an entire chapter to the circulation of discourse about the Litvinenko poisoning.

Macgilchrist reports:

"Recent journalism scholarship suggests that, although it is rarely acknowledged in the press, news stories often stem from press releases and news agency services. A study of domestic news in the UK's quality press by Justin Lewis and colleagues found that 80 percent of stories were to some extent based on such material although only 1 percent of stories were directly attributed to news agencies and none to press releases. (Lewis, Williams and Franklin 2008a: 5, 15). A study in Germany found that almost two thirds of the news media (television, press, radio, agencies) were based on PR materials in the 1980s (Baerns 1991; cf. Rus-Mohl 2003)." (See *Journalism and the Political* for references.)

Macgilchrist gives as an example the way in which news reports defined and discussed thallium in the Litvinenko case. There was a period of time when stories focused on thallium as the agent that poisoned Litvinenko. She sees a common thread among the reports.

According to my dictionary, thallium is "a sparsely but widely distributed poisonous metallic element that resembles lead in physical properties and is used chiefly in the form of compounds in photoelectric cells or as a pesticide." But Macgilshrist points out, "Although no press release was ever mentioned in the newspapers, there are indications that various news stories are drawn from one source text, for example in the explanation of thallium, the poison initially thought to have poisoned Litvinenko."

She cites the following examples:

"...reports last night suggested tests had confirmed the presence of the poison thallium, a colourless and odourless liquid often used to kill rats." —The *Observer*, 19 November 2006

"Mr. Litvinenko is thought to have been poisoned with thallium, a colourless and odourless liquid that is often used to kill rats." —The *Sunday Telegraph*, 19 November 2006

"...it is thought to have been thallium, a highly-toxic colourless and odourless poison, used to kill rats." —The *Sunday Express*, 19 November 2006

The use of a common source seems very evident here. It doesn't seem to be a dictionary definition. Was the common source a wire service such as AP or Reuters? Or was it a press release that was part of the managed story? I don't know, but I found a November 20 AP story that called thallium a "toxic metal." And in a November 23 story, Reuters called thallium a "heavy metal."

The stories that Litvinenko's death was an assassination by the Russian state tend to include the theory that poison was slipped into his tea at a hotel bar. The term "heavy metal" doesn't "sound" like something that would go unnoticed in one's tea. But the "colourless and odourless" liquid conveniently fits better with the story's theme.

Macgilchrist also points to replicative phrases that compare Litvinenko with Georgi Markov, a Bulgarian murdered with a poisonous pellet shot into his body, and also passages that contend "there is no suggestion" that a sushi restaurant where Litvinenko had dined was in any way complicit.

Confirmatory Analysis

The large scale of this story seems to confirm that there was a managed story afoot. I don't think that normal and good editorial judgment would have accorded the level of importance to this story that it received.

Keep in mind that Litvinenko's name wasn't exactly a household word. Why would anyone care about his accusations? He was relatively unknown. The Russians have a phrase for this: "Shiroko izvesten v uzkih krugah" — i.e., he was widely known in narrow circles. That's a far cry from being a global newsmaker.

And on top of that, the Litvinenko theories seemed illogical and fantastical. It's really hard to see how genuine editorial judgment would have propelled that story to such heights.

Not Just Litvinenko

The mysterious replication of themes in Russia-related news coverage does not seem to have been limited to the Litvinenko case. Over the years there also have been a number of examples where negative, counter-factual stories that have been spread widely in the international press appear to have had a common origin.

The "gas as a weapon" theme is a good example. On January 9, 2009, the *Los Angeles Times* ran an editorial with the headline, "Kremlin uses gas as a weapon." The article explains that it "looks like a calculated strategy by Russia to regain influence over countries that were once part of the Soviet empire and to neutralize European opposition." It dismisses the fact that the incident arose from Ukraine's non-payment of its gas bill. Ukraine claims it was disputing a hike in the price of natural gas. And along with the multitude of other news reports on this theme, the *LA Times* neglected to point out that Russia is being called upon to boost its energy prices to market levels as part of its accession to the

World Trade Organization. And so it was with similar "gas-as-a-weapon" stories carried by other outlets.

Then there were the "Russia Invades Georgia" stories. They were top worldwide stories for some time. But when unmistakable conclusions were reached that it actually was Georgia that shot first, the coverage was far less robust. Were the original reports part of someone's managed story? As with the "gas-as-a-weapon" theme, it sure looks like it. But I've not dug into these issues in depth.

The Free Press Crackdown

An issue that I have followed very closely is that of Russian press freedom. And, in all candor, I have to tell you that most of what you've heard about it in the Western press is false. The "free press crackdown" theme is specious.

The usual theme of the coverage is, "Putin has cracked down on Russia's independent media." That's certainly gets attention. But, when you look into the facts, you find a very different story. When Putin took office, Russia had no independent media. Virtually no media outlets were free to offer consumers honest, reliable news.

Laws instituted during the Yeltsin era didn't allow media outlets to achieve the financial success needed to operate freely and independently. That's what thrust them into the clutches of oligarchs, governors, mayors, and others who put money into the loss-making media ventures in return for the opportunity to distort the news in their own favor, and to use the media as a weapon against competitors and the Kremlin itself.

A lot of the stories confuse pluralism in the media with the kind of press freedom that's needed to enable an informed citizenry in a democratic society. People need sources of reliable news, not a cacophony of distortions. Certainly, plurality will exist whenever the press is free.

But, pluralism in itself is not a sure sign of press freedom. You know, often it's said that "a wet nose is a sign of a healthy dog." But, you can't rub water on your sick dog's nose and make him well. Likewise, applying pluralism to the subjugated media of the Yeltsin years didn't create press freedom — it was just an illusion.

Putin's Killing Journalists

The tragic murders of so many journalists in Russia also have been a rallying cause for fact-deficit journalism and activism. The January 23, 2007 edition of the *Moscow Times* reported, "A high-level delegation from the New York-based Committee to Protect Journalists called on Monday for the Russian government to step up its efforts to solve a rash of killings that it says have made this country one of the world's most dangerous for journalists." Their request was certainly laudable, and I'm glad that CPJ made this effort. But, this theme has spawned a lot of terrible journalism:

—Trudy Rubin writing for the *Philadelphia Inquirer* remarked on the Politkovskaya murder: "She's the 13th Russian journalist killed in a contract-style murder since Russian President Vladimir Putin took office in 2000. This vicious killing is a reminder of how far Russia has swerved back toward authoritarianism under Putin."

—CBS News reported: "As the European Union and the U.S. demanded a thorough probe into Saturday's contract-style killing, there was skepticism that the authorities would ever uncover the culprits of the latest in a series of killings of journalists in Russia under President Vladimir Putin, who has been increasingly accused of rolling back post-Soviet freedoms since coming to power in 2000."

—Even the above-referenced *Moscow Times* story quotes a distortion: "Since President Vladimir Putin came to power in 2000, 40 journalists' murders have not been satisfactorily solved, the International Federation of Journalists announced this month." There was no mention in the story that most of those killings occurred under Yeltsin and went unsolved throughout his tenure in office.

The CPJ delegation had lamented a "rash of killings." But, according to its own website at the time, in the 7 years before Putin was elected, there were 30 journalist murders. In the 7 years since he took office, there had been 14 such murders as of mid-2006. In other words, under Putin, the number of journalists murdered each year has been significantly reduced.

Isn't it quite distasteful that the deaths of these journalists have been politicized in these ways?

And by the way, at the time of his death, Litvinenko was indeed a working journalist himself, filing regular stories with the Chechen Press State News Agency. The Committee to Protect Journalists maintains a database of journalist deaths. One would expect that Litvinenko would have been recorded as a journalist death in the UK. But it wasn't recorded at all.

Was this just an oversight? The media certainly didn't emphasize that Litvinenko was a journalist. But, how could CPJ have missed one of the most conspicuous journalist deaths of the century? I know we're talking about the politically-charged Litvinenko case here, but I hope that CPJ's oversight isn't for some kind of sinister reason. Nonetheless, it seems very odd. Maybe they'll correct their oversight now.

Ineffectual PR Response

It seems that in this case the media's dirty little secret has resulted in negative coverage for Putin and Russia. Putin certainly appears to have been tarred and feathered in the international press over and over again. And at least to some extent, that has happened with the help of managed stories.

It's been reported that Putin has spent tons of money on Western PR agencies trying to improve his and Russia's image abroad. But instead of helping to clean up the tar and feathers, based on the results so far, it looks like they just fleeced him.

Chapter 7
More Mysterious Themes

They just keep on coming.

THE flip side of the "Putin did it" theme is one that accuses Boris Berezovsky of having engineered the murders of Litvinenko and Politkovskaya just to embarrass Putin.

Circumstantial evidence for this theory is offered by outlets, citing that both tragedies were related to dates of significance for Putin: (1) Politkovskaya was murdered on his birthday. (2) The media blitz over Litvinenko occurred as Putin posed in ceremonial garb for the official group portrait at the Asia Pacific Economic Cooperation meeting in Hanoi.

I could find no real evidence in media reports to tie Berezovsky to either the Litvinenko or Politkovskaya murders.

And, while the timing of the Litvinenko media blitz may make one wonder if Berezovsky called on his PR connections opportunistically, that is certainly no reason to conclude complicity in the poisoning.

Berezovsky in the News

But some media outlets disagreed about the "embarrass Putin" theory. On one hand a November 28 item about Litvinenko in the *Telegraph* was headlined, "Was he sacrificed to embarrass Putin?" The article said this is the most popular theory in Moscow, and suggested that "Berezovsky has not escaped suspicion."

However, on December 15, *Kommersant* wrote that "there is no dominant opinion on the matter among the public." It backed up that claim with a Levada Center poll that also indicated only 15 percent suspect Berezovsky of the crime.

Amid all that disagreement, there is one aspect of this controversial angle that has been settled. And it's been settled in a court of law:

All-Russian State Television and Radio Broadcasting Company (VGTRK) broadcast in May 2007 a program that accused Berezovsky of being responsible for the poisoning of Litvinenko. Berezovsky brought a libel action against the Russian TV broadcaster, and won. In rendering a verdict, the judge said, "I can say unequivocally that there is no evidence before me that Mr. Berezovsky had any part in the murder of Mr. Litvinenko. Nor, for that matter, do I see any basis for reasonable grounds to suspect him of it".

Other Themes

Since Litvinenko's death, a couple of other themes have emerged to explain it. One is that Litvinenko had been involved in trafficking polonium. It could have been with or without his knowledge. But the result was, as the stories go, that Litvinenko accidently became contaminated.

As the 5th anniversary of Litvinenko's death approached, another theory popped up. An October 13, 2011 story in the *Telegraph* was headlined, "Alexander Litvinenko may have committed suicide, says Russian suspect." That suspect described in the article is Andrei Lugovoi.

Chapter 8
Friends and Enigmatic Connections

Litvinenko certainly wasn't short of friends!

FRIENDS. In almost all news accounts, the people connected to Alexander Litvinenko were referred to as his friends. I did a Google search on Litvinenko friends, and got the following list:

—Yuri Shvets, former KGB major

—Akhmed Zakayev, foreign minister of the Chechen Republic government-in-exile, and Litvinenko neighbor

—Oleg Gordievsky, former KGB colonel now living in Great Britain

—Vladimir Bukovsky, former soviet dissident, author, and human rights activist

—Boris Berezovsky, Russian-born billionaire now enjoying political asylum in Great Britain

—Andrei Nekrasov, a Russian film and TV director from St. Petersburg

—Alexander Goldfarb, a Russian microbiologist formerly employed by George Soros, and now a civil liberties activist for Berezovsky, based in New York

—Paul Joyal, an American security analyst who was shot and wounded after commenting on the Litvinenko case on American TV

—Mario Scaramella, an Italian lawyer and security consultant, sometimes called an academic

—Anna Politkovskaya, murdered Russian journalist and political activist.

Just Friends?

Didn't Litvinenko have business relationships with some of these people? A few stories referred to Dmitry Kovtun, Andrei Lugovoi, Mario Scaramella, and Yuri Shvets as business associates. But, in most reports, Litvinenko had only friends.

Isn't that strange that the story was so consistently reported in this idiosyncratic way?

If some of these "friends" also represented business relationships, wouldn't knowing that have expanded readers' understanding of what was going on here?

More Than Friends

Boris Berezovsky admitted that he had been Litvinenko's employer. He told CBS News, "Yeah, initially he worked just for me."

BBC reported that Berezovsky owns the house that Litvinenko was living in. Berezovsky affirmed that himself in late March 2007 when he was interrogated by Scotland Yard. (A transcript was posted on *Kommersant's* website in May 2007.) He also admitted that he is paying for Litvinenko's son to attend private school. During the interrogation, he told investigators that there came a time when "Sasha [Litvinenko's nickname] went to another job." No mention was made of what that job was.

After the job change, however, Berezovsky said, Litvinenko did not routinely inform him about the content of his investigations. No mention was made of the nature of the investigations either.

Nonetheless, Berezovsky did describe a Litvinenko investigation concerning the Alfa Group (a financial-industrial conglomerate) and its president Mikhail Fridman. Berezovsky said that Litvinenko believed that "the group could pose a threat to our lives."

Interestingly, Fridman's name had arisen in August 2006 in connection with Berezovsky. Radio Free Europe/Radio Liberty reported, "A close associate of Russian tycoon Boris Berezovsky has claimed that Ukrainian parliament speaker Oleksander Moroz plotted with Mikhail Fridman, the head of Alfa Group, to kill Ukrainian journalist Heorhiy Gongadze in September 2000."

The RFE/RL story continues: "Speaking at a press conference in Kyiv on August 1, Goldfarb distributed the text of an affidavit by an unnamed U.S. citizen, in which that person claims that Moroz, a member of parliament in September 2000, met with Fridman and a number of suspected Russian criminal bosses from the 'Izmailovskaya' gang in Moscow to plan Gongadze's killing." RFE/RL also noted that, "Goldfarb provided little evidence for the latest accusations."

So this story claims that Litvinenko had cautioned Berezovsky about Fridman. Then, we find that a Berezovsky associate had been accusing Fridman of plotting murder. That Berezovsky associate turns out to be Alexander Goldfarb. You'll find his name on the above list of Litvinenko's friends. Indeed, many reports refer to Goldfarb as the Litvinenko family spokesman.

Another strange coincidence emanates from a November 19, 2006 *Daily Mail* report. It claims Litvinenko "made corruption allegations against billionaire Chelsea owner Roman Abramovich." Now, in 2011, Litvinenko's friend Berezovsky is involved in a $5 billion law suit against Abramovich. On October 18, the Guardian reported: "Earlier this month [Litvinenko's widow, Marina] turned up to support Berezovsky in his colourful legal battle against fellow oligarch Roman Abramovich."

What does all this have to do with Alexander Litvinenko's poisoning? Perhaps nothing at all. But, the chain of relationships is certainly interesting, and would have been worthy of coverage.

Friends. What a dizzying circle of friends.

Investigations

Another thing that Boris Berezovsky had told CBS News is that "he had recently reduced his financial support of Litvinenko." The *Guardian Observer* (December 3, 2006) quoted Julia Svetlichnaya, a university graduate student who was writing a book about the Chechen conflict, as saying Litvinenko told her that he was short of money.

But, that's not all that Svetlichnaya had to say about Litvinenko. The same CBS News item that quoted Berezovsky above (a January 7, 2007 *60 Minutes* program), also quoted Svetlichnaya extensively on Litvinenko: "He told me that, at the moment, he's doing a project for blackmailing one of the Russian oligarchs which resides in UK," she said. "He thought that it was actually an OK thing to do because this particular person, as Litvinenko claimed, had a connection with the Kremlin, had a connection with Putin. And so in his view, it was OK to blackmail him." She told a similar story to the *Guardian Observer*: "He told me he was going to blackmail or sell sensitive information about all kinds of powerful people including oligarchs, corrupt officials and sources in the Kremlin." Perhaps these were the "investigations" that Berezovsky said Litvinenko had not shared with him?

According to a couple of Russia-related blogs, the *Sunday Times* (London) suggested on December 10 that Svetlichnaya was part of a Kremlin campaign aimed at discrediting Litvinenko.

But then, on February 18, 2007, came the following correction from the *Times*: "Our report on the investigation into the death of Alexander Litvinenko ('Kremlin wants to quiz exiles', December 10) referred to reports that Julia Svetlichnaja, a researcher at the Centre for the Study of Democracy at Westminster University, may have been part of a Kremlin-orchestrated campaign to discredit Mr. Litvinenko and said it was believed that she had previously worked for a state-owned Russian company. We are happy to make it clear that Ms. Svetlichnaja has never worked for a state-owned Russian company and we accept that she was not part of any Kremlin-inspired campaign to discredit Mr. Litvinenko. We apologise for any distress our report caused her."

Interestingly, the copy of that story

("Kremlin wants to quiz exiles") on the
Times' website no longer contains any
reference to Svetlichnaya.

Chapter 9
Hard-to-Classify Curiosities

They lead from London to the halls of the U.S. Congress.

HERE are a few more oddities about the Litvinenko case:

Litvinenko Was a Journalist?

As mentioned in the previous chapter, Alexander Litvinenko was a journalist. I'm not referring to his role in writing a book about Putin. He was an actual, working journalist with the Chechen Press State News Agency. Between May 7, 2005, and October 24, 2006, just 8 days before the poisoning, the Chechen Press agency carried 26 bylined stories of Litvinenko's. They are datelined London where, by the time of his poisoning, he had become a British citizen.

Why was this occupational activity overlooked in the news stories about Litvinenko? There was more than adequate attention paid to what he used to be, i.e., a security services worker. Why didn't journalists pick up on the fact that Litvinenko was a fellow journalist?

It doesn't seem like that's all he was, though. The question still remains regarding what else Litvinenko did. Having some facts about that might have given news audiences more context regarding his fate than the seemingly endless repetition about his supposed previous "spy" occupation.

But He Wasn't a Spy!

Countless media reports referred to Litvinenko as a "former KGB spy." That's been the case not only in this poisoning story, but also in coverage of Litvinenko's litany of earlier accusations against Putin.

But then I heard from a well-informed former lecturer at the FSB Academy in whom I have considerable confidence. His students worked with Litvinenko in the mid 1990s. According to my source, Litvinenko never was a spy and never worked for the KGB! He told me that Litvinenko had been an investigative officer in a prison before joining the FSB. All of his professional life he specialized in organized crime. When he did join the FSB, he was assigned to a joint unit with the Ministry of Interior.

Do the media have a reliable source for the

"spy" designator? If they do, they didn't share that with their audiences. Maybe this is another example of those self-validating facts that aren't factual.

The Riddle of John Henry

London toxicologist Dr. John Henry seems to have popped onto the scene around November 19. A BBC report of that date says, "Clinical toxicologist John Henry, who examined Mr. Litvinenko on Saturday [November 18], told the BBC he believes he [Litvinenko] was given a potentially lethal dose of thallium."

The *Telegraph* chimed in with, "The *Sunday Telegraph* has learnt that he [Litvinenko] was examined in hospital by Professor John Henry, a British toxicologist..."

(Just as an aside, that *Telegraph* article also refers to Litvinenko as "the 50 year old." Actually, he was 43 or 44. The article also talks of Litvinenko meeting "a female journalist at Itsu." Litvinenko's interlocutor at that Japanese restaurant is widely accepted to have been a male named Mario Scaramella. He's been variously described as an academic, a lawyer, or as a security consultant, but not as a journalist. This *Telegraph* article seems noteworthy as an example of very sloppy journalism.)

In *Journalism and the Political*, Dr. Macgilchrist does an extensive analysis of the coverage that refers to Henry. Her analysis points to the role that making reference to "an expert of good standing" can play in press releases. She calls such references an important ingredient in getting PR material imported directly into media news stories.

Macgilchrist cites various ways of referring to Henry, including: "Britain's leading poison specialist," "a world expert on poisons," "a clinical toxicologist at Imperial College London."

The November 20th London *Times* reported, "John Henry, a clinical toxicologist who examined Mr. Litvinenko on Saturday, said that the former spy was quite seriously sick."

Macgilchrist also calls attention to the ways media outlets described Henry's relationship with Litvinenko. She cites references such as "his patient," "his toxicologist," and "one of his medical team." What's more, Henry was also characterized as "treating Litvinenko," "advising on Mr. Litvinenko's treatment," "overseeing Mr. Litvinenko's treatment."

But then, on November 24th, the *Guardian* ran a report that in effect says none of that is true:

"A leading toxicologist, Professor John Henry, was contacted by a friend of the sick Russian and spoke of his fears that the former spy had been poisoned with thallium, a heavy metal, or with a radioactive substance, theories which have since been ruled out. Prof. Henry had not been treating Mr. Litvinenko, however, and the hospital says he had not seen any of the test results when he first raised his theories in media interviews."

How weird is that? Henry wasn't even an official part of the case. He was brought in by "friends" and then let loose on the press!

The Litvinenko matter keeps getting more fantastical and fantastical, curiouser and curiouser.

It's getting hard to believe anything about the case, especially that which comes out of

London.

Source of Polonium

Soon after polonium was implicated in the Litvinenko poisoning, media started connecting it with Russia. On November 24, the *Telegraph* alleged that polonium 210 "is rarely used outside military and scientific establishments and requires professional expertise." On the 25th while reporting on the polonium angle, it reported "Security chiefs are alarmed at the possibility that Russia may be prepared to strike at critics with little care for its public image." The story called polonium a "rare and deadly substance." And by December 16, the *Telegraph* ran the headline, "Russian unit may have got polonium to kill Litvinenko."

So far this sounds like a pretty convincing indictment, doesn't it?

But in this Litvinenko fantasyland, it's worth reality testing those claims.

In a March 19, 2008 *New York Sun* article entitled "The Specter that Haunts the Death of Litvinenko," journalist Edward Jay Epstein identifies Alexander Goldfarb, the

Berezovsky associate, as a source of some of this information. "A scientist by training, Mr. Goldfarb authoritatively asserted in his book 'Death of a Dissident,' written with Marina Litvinenko, that '97 percent of the known production of polonium ... takes place in Russia.'"

Epstein continues, "Since little else had been written about this rare isotope, many commentators assumed it was an established fact." But, Epstein points out, "To make that determination, it is necessary to know both how much polonium 210 is produced in Russia and how much is produced in other countries. Yet, as polonium 210 production is a closely guarded secret, neither quantity is known." Epstein observes that in 2006, no country, including Russia, was admitting to manufacturing any polonium at all.

Former Russian nuclear minister Evgeny Adamov explains that polonium is not difficult to manufacture, and that it can be done even by a layman without a background in chemistry. He also claims that traces of polonium can be found anywhere, even in food. "I dare say you could find polonium in a piece of bread. But in such concentrations it is not hazardous to health," Adamov added. He said only direct contact with polonium or its vapors will be dangerous.

Now, some readers may be thinking that that's just the Russian version of things.

But on December 3, 2006, the *New York Times* ran a story headlined, "Polonium, $22.50 Plus Tax." The story talks of "the relative ubiquity of polonium 210" in products that are readily available. It quotes William Happer, a physicist at Princeton and an advisor to the U.S. government on nuclear forensics, "You can get it all over the place."

Explaining the $22.50 angle, the *Times* goes on, "Commercially, websites and companies sell many products based on polonium 210, with labels warning of health dangers. By some estimates, a lethal dose might cost as little as $22.50, plus tax. 'Radiation from polonium is dangerous if the solid material is ingested or inhaled,' warns the label of an antistatic brush. 'Keep away from children.'"

But could that polonium be weaponized? The *Times* reports, "Manufacturers of antistatic devices take great pains to make the polonium hard to remove. Even so, Dr.

Zimmerman of King's College said it could be done with 'careful lab work,' which he declined to describe."

The Russian polonium connection seems to just have gone up in smoke.

Was the U.S. Congress Duped?

That smoke wasn't seen in the halls of the U.S. Congress, though. According to the House Foreign Affairs Committee, in April 2008 the House "passed a measure, introduced by [Ileana] Ros-Lehtinen, expressing the sense of Congress that the fatal radiation poisoning of Alexander Litvinenko raises significant concerns about the potential involvement of the Russian authorities in Mr. Litvinenko's death and about the security and proliferation of radioactive materials. 97% percent [sic] of the world's legal production of polonium 210 occurs in Russia."

But Ros-Lehtinen didn't stop there. According to a November 24, 2010 release from the Committee, "Ros-Lehtinen calls for withdrawal of U.S.-Russia nuclear cooperation agreement pending further investigation of Litvinenko murder."

The release states, "New reports that the extremely rare radioactive material used in the murder of Alexander Litvinenko may have been of Russian origin raise further questions about the Russian government's possible role in the murder."

Ros-Lehtinen herself said, "I strongly urge President Obama to withdraw the U.S.-Russia nuclear cooperation agreement and block any purchase of U.S. nuclear resources by Russia's Rosatom or its subsidiaries until these new allegations about possible involvement by Russia's civilian nuclear agency in the radioactive poisoning of Litvinenko have been thoroughly investigated."

I've presented this Ros-Lehtinen information not to call attention to her ignorance, but to highlight the dangerous ramifications of pervasively bad journalism. Since January 3, 2011, Ros-Lehtinen has been chairman of the House Foreign Affairs Committee.

This is a good example of how all the Litvinenko-related fantasy and illogic turns scary!

Chapter 10
The Yeltsin Scandal

The media saw this one differently.

WHILE considering the media's treatment of the Litvinenko poisoning, it is interesting to contrast it with how they handled the Yeltsin scandal:

A stone drunk Boris Yeltsin stood across from the White House in Washington. He was there in his underwear hailing a taxi. In his stupor, Yeltsin just wanted to go out for a pizza.

That bizarre incident from the 1990s made the news in 2009. A PR blitz for a book by Taylor Branch about the Clinton presidency seems to have propelled the story.

But those Yeltsin antics of inebriation aren't the scandal here. Indeed, the 2009 story was not actually news. The whole tale had been told earlier by Strobe Talbott in his book on Clinton presidential diplomacy. It was released in 2002 and garnered media attention back then.

So then what is the "Yeltsin Scandal"? The

crux of it is the Western press' inexplicably lenient treatment of the Yeltsin presidency, especially in comparison to his successors'.

It's Another Bizarre Story

As a media professional, I've followed with interest the press coverage of the recent Russian presidents: Boris Yeltsin, Vladimir Putin, Dmitry Medvedev. And, I have to admit that I've found the nature of the coverage itself to be yet another bizarre story, one with mystery and intrigue of its own.

Over the years, Yeltsin has been characterized variously as a hero who brought down communism, as the foremost proponent of Russia's transformation to democracy and a market economy, and as a stalwart of Russia's free press.

Beyond that popular imagery, however, there was a less attractive side. Yeltsin presided over a looting of state assets that created a circle of newly-minted tycoons that helped to protect Yeltsin. In addition, acting against the constitution, Yeltsin dismissed the duly elected parliament. And when the members refused to go, he brought in tanks to shell the parliament building in a confrontation that ultimately claimed approximately 150 lives. Somehow he was able to win reelection in a contest where he held roughly a 5 percent approval rating going into the election season. Ultimately, Yeltsin led the country into a financial collapse near the end of his presidency.

Admiring Boris

Yeltsin is nevertheless used in many media accounts and in political discourse as a standard of accomplishment against which his successors are being compared. Notably, Putin is criticized widely in the media for rolling back the democratic gains of the Yeltsin era, for reversing the course Yeltsin had taken away from Soviet-era autocratic rule, and for clamping down on Russia's free press. Typical headlines include "The Rollback of Democracy in Vladimir Putin's Russia" (*Washington Post*) and "How Putin Muzzled Russia's Free Press" (*Wall Street Journal*).

According to my analysis, media accounts seem generally to advance a Yeltsin persona that combines hero, fierce democratic and market reformer, and relatively harmless drunk. President Bill Clinton has been quoted as observing, "We can't ever forget that Yeltsin drunk is better than most of the alternatives sober."

Putin's persona in the press, however, is more that of a suspicious, power-hungry autocrat who will stop at nothing, not even murder. On the PBS *News Hour with Jim Lehrer*, Senator John McCain once accused Putin's Kremlin of instituting a "state-run kind of Mussolini style government."

A Closer Look at Yeltsin

As a case-in-point, I examined the *New York Times* coverage of Yeltsin's shelling of the parliament in 1993. That was one of Yeltsin's most egregious acts. The *Times* ran a story entitled "SHOWDOWN IN MOSCOW: Tactics; Yeltsin Attack Strategy: Bursts Followed by Lulls." Here are some excerpts illustrating how the *Times* covered the story:

"The assault on the Russian Parliament building today was a textbook example of the decisive application of military power...

"And as the daylong assault went on, it was clear that Mr. Yeltsin's commanders had decided on gradualism...

"The Russian troops were looking for Bolshoi Devyatinsky lane ... where the defiant lawmakers had maintained their headquarters...

"With the outcome of the battle never in doubt, the clear preference of the military was to scare the anti-Yeltsin demonstrators into surrendering and to limit casualties...

"The only question was the number of lives that would be lost. And that was largely left up to the rebels as they were alternately bombarded with shells and appeals to surrender."

Just note how soft this coverage is. I'm not taking sides on whether Yeltsin's actions were appropriate or not. But, the Yeltsin side is characterized as valiant and measured.

The other side is characterized as defiant and to blame for its own fate. The story has a factual basis. The president really did launch a tank assault on the parliament. However, the circumstances clearly seem to be spun in a way that tempers that stark reality.

The Outcome?

Now you have a better picture of the Yeltsin scandal. As you can see, it isn't about the then-president of Russia. It is really about the media and how they have covered Yeltsin.

But, what ever happened to Yeltsin's drunken pizza escapade? According to Bill Clinton, "Yeltsin got his pizza."

Chapter 11
The Putin Scandal

Laying the groundwork for what's next to come.

THE Putin scandal actually started during the Yeltsin administration.

Indeed, the seeds of the scandal began to germinate during the mid 1990s, back when Putin was still part of the city administration in St. Petersburg.

I first learned about it after reading a Sense of Congress resolution that had been introduced by then-Representative Thomas Lantos of California.

It was a scathing attack on Boris Yeltsin's media policies. While those policies were indeed worthy of criticism, the rabid rhetoric of the Lantos resolution sounded like it must have been talking about the days of Stalin.

So, I called Lantos' office and asked his legislative assistant where they got that stuff from. The only answer I received was that "the Congressman feels very strongly about that issue." Even when I tried to probe deeper, I just got the same answer.

Fast Forward

About a year later, I was meeting with a staffer at the Senate Committee on Foreign Relations, and I asked her if she knew anything about that Lantos resolution. She wrote the name "Don Bonker" on a piece of paper and suggested that I contact him.

After some research, I found that he was a former congressman from the state of Washington, now working for Apco, the large Washington, DC-based lobbying and PR firm. I called him on the phone and asked him if he was involved in drafting the resolution. He said yes. I asked him who his client was. He said, Vladimir Gusinsky.

Vladimir Who?

Gusinsky is a former Russian media tycoon and former owner of the TV network NTV. In 2000 he was jailed for fraud. Eventually, the charges were dropped. Upon release from jail, he fled Russia and has been living outside the country ever since.

Why was he involved in an American Sense of Congress resolution? As I put the whole story together in retrospect, what appears to have happened is this: Yeltsin was incensed over how he was being portrayed on NTV's *Kukly* program, a satirical puppet show.

Requests of Gusinsky to knock it off were dismissed. So then, Yeltsin had the prosecutor general bring charges against Gusinsky for embarrassing the president.

Apparently, Gusinsky retaliated by having Lantos introduce the Congressional resolution which implied that if Yeltsin didn't shape up with regard to media policy, the United States might question the financial support it was giving Yeltsin.

The upshot was that Gusinsky won. Yeltsin fired the prosecutor general, the charges were dropped, and Yeltsin appeared publicly embracing his kukla (puppet).

But Where's Putin?

To this point, Putin wasn't involved yet in his own scandal. His entrance came when Yeltsin appointed him as prime minister and heir apparent to the presidency. While Berezovsky, the other major media mogul, was initially supportive of Putin, Gusinsky was not.

Here are a couple of snippets that I found from Gusinsky's newspaper *Segodnya*:

—"For Putin any coherent economic policy is a mirage."

—"...voters will hardly vote for a president who moves into the Kremlin over the corpses of his soldiers in Grozny,"

The *Washington Times* reported, "Yulia Latynina, a columnist for the journal *Segodnya*, said behind-the-scenes Kremlin maneuvering to undermine the acting president's most serious challengers was designed to leave voters with just one item on the menu: 'the oatmeal named Putin.'"

And, the *Chicago Sun-Times* said *Segodnya* editor Leonid Radzhikovsky told them, "No one feared Yeltsin, but many fear Putin."

Throughout the international press, Putin was variously referred to as "former KGB, master of backroom intrigue, the gray cardinal of St. Petersburg," "a Cold War KGB spy in Germany," a "46-year-old former KGB spy," a "laconic, unsmiling ex-KGB official," and an "unheralded former KGB agent."

A Boston University professor was quoted in the media asking, "In what normal country does one go to the secret services to appoint a new prime minister?"

Now, more than 10 years after these reports, it's hard to trace the exact extent that Gusinsky's news activities may have influenced the broader coverage. But, it's also hard to read over those Putin characterizations without thinking back on Gusinsky's proficiency in shaping perceptions.

And the world's perceptions of Putin were certainly shaped then. He was virtually unknown internationally before Yeltsin made him prime minister.

The Scandal Defined

There is a stark difference between the cited descriptions of Putin and the characterizations of Yeltsin that were quoted in the previous chapter. And that is the crux of the Putin scandal. Media coverage flipped from a whitewash of Yeltsin to a vilification of Putin.

Some people believe that this is part of a conspiracy among the Western media to put Russia in an unfavorable light. Others simply write off the negative coverage to lingering Cold War animosities. But neither of those theories can account for the great disparity between the Yeltsin coverage and the Putin stories. This is another scandal of media failing to deliver reliably honest news to their consumers.

Cooking the News

The Gusinsky matter represents a good case study in how the media can be spun in a direction that seems contrary to the facts.

According to Russian media expert Alexei Pankin, during the Yeltsin presidency "Gusinsky received over one billion dollars in loans from state-controlled sources to build Most Media, the parent company of his network, NTV. But, when in 2001 he defaulted, his business manager estimated that the company was worth circa $200 million. What about the difference between $1 billion plus loans and $200 million? What happened to that money?"

Under the new Putin presidency, Gusinsky

was charged with fraud. But, somehow Gusinsky's media outlets were portrayed in the West as paragons of press freedom. The actions against Gusinsky were characterized as a retreat from press freedom.

From what I could see, that was absolutely counter-factual. You can't retreat from a press freedom that wasn't there in the first place. Based on the little advertising I could see in his newspaper, *Segodnya*, it literally had no visible means of support. And that is typical for all too many Russian media outlets.

Financial self-sufficiency is an essential ingredient of a truly free press. Loss-making media outlets supported by entities bent on influencing the news tend to become indentured to their benefactors' point of view. Being indentured and being free are mutually exclusive states.

But the furor over Putin's purported clamp-down on Gusinsky's "free press" led to Gusinsky's release from jail. That's when he up and fled Russia for parts West.

(Note: It is widely said that the kinds of offenses for which Gusinsky was accused were accepted practices during the Yeltsin years. Berezovsky concurred. Calling for blanket amnesty, he remarked, "Only those people who have been asleep for the past 10 years have avoided willingly or unwillingly breaking the law.")

The Loss of Press Freedom

To this day, news stories bemoan the loss of the press freedom of Yeltsin's day. Pankin, however, compares the media of that era to a "remarkable flower called the Victoria Regia. It grows in Brazil. From a distance you see a huge beautiful flower. Then you realize that it has no roots and can only survive in the hard-to-replicate environment of tropical marshes. And, finally, when you really get up close, you find that it stinks!"

I think Pankin's got it right.

The Putin scandal seems to have been a triumph of the "managed story" over reality.

Chapter 12
The Deathbed Accusation

Something's fishy here.

FOLLOWING Alexander Litvinenko's death, a statement attributed to him appeared. It expressed gratitude to many of those who had touched his life. And it went on to express contempt for "the person responsible for my present condition," subsequently identified in the statement as "Mr. Putin." BBC reported on November 24, that the statement had been "read out by his friend Alex Goldfarb outside University College Hospital, London."

CNN and the London *Times* reported the statement had been dictated by Litvinenko. The *Washington Post* called it "...a statement Litvinenko's family and friends said he dictated on his deathbed." NBC News in its March 14, 2007 *Dateline* program referred to it as "an extraordinary letter that Litvinenko had written to President Putin from his deathbed." I don't want to make too much of a small point, but this illuminates the kind of sloppy or inaccurate journalism that has plagued the Litvinenko story.

The *Washington Post* deserves credit on this one for attributing the characterization of the statement to "family and friends." The NBC News claim that it was a letter written to Putin seems to be the epitome of inattention to detail.

But, the overarching issue is that, on its surface, the Litvinenko statement doesn't sound like something that was just dictated on a deathbed. It is in English, and was in typed format. It appears to be signed by hand, with the day of the month inserted by hand also. Why should that be significant? First of all, Alexander Litvinenko was not extremely proficient in English. The Frontline Club in London, a media organization whose slogan is "championing independent journalism," hosted Litvinenko as a speaker shortly before he was poisoned. At that meeting he began his remarks, "My name is Alexander Litvinenko. I am former KGB and FSB officer. Ah, Mine ah, my difficult, ah my speech is difficult for me. Can I use translator?"

Compare that with the eloquent language of the "deathbed" statement.

Of course, it may have been spoken in

Russian and then translated into English. The point of this discussion, however, is simply that it doesn't sound like an off-the-cuff statement of any kind. And, media audiences deserved to have had questions asked by journalists about the circumstances surrounding the statement: Had Litvinenko been assisted in composing the statement? If so, who helped? And in what way? Those answers might have helped audiences to judge whether the statement's content purely represented Litvinenko's agenda, or if it perhaps served someone else's ends.

I made these points in presenting my report at the World Congress of the International Federation of Journalists in Moscow.

Epilogue: In the wake of that presentation, it now appears that the Berezovsky camp has abandoned the contention that the statement really had been dictated by Litvinenko. The new version is that the statement actually had been written by Alexander Goldfarb who read it to Litvinenko, who then said, "I agree with every word of it."

It seems that the deathbed accusation has started to unravel.

Chapter 13
Litvinenko Redux

Getting up to date.

AS of October 2011, the coroner in London has not ruled Litvinenko's death to be a homicide.

Indeed, no certification has been issued as to the cause and manner of death.

Nonetheless, since 2006, news reports have referred to Litvinenko's death as a murder.

But now, recent word from the coroner's office has set the record straight. What many have reported as fact is not an established finding. There's never been a definitive determination that Alexander Litvinenko was murdered. This startling fact turned up as I was preparing this book.

Rebirth of Inaccurate Reports

Coincidentally, in October 2011, the Litvinenko story started to reemerge.

A new volley of headlines includes:

"Russia murdered Litvinenko, says top prosecutor," —The *Sunday Times* (London), October 2

"Alexander Litvinenko murder was 'London nuclear terror,'" —BBC News, October 13

"Litvinenko coroner to examine if Russian state behind killing," —The *Telegraph*, October 13

All these headlines seem to assert that Litvinenko was in fact murdered. Perhaps the most egregious headline is that of the *Sunday Times*. It appears to be claiming that a top prosecutor has accused Russia of murdering Litvinenko.

What the headline neglects to mention is the fact that this "top prosecutor" is a former prosecutor who is now a lawyer with Matrix Chambers. According to his official bio, his practice includes "business and corporate crime and associated extraditions, financial regulation, market abuse, terrorism, human rights, and media law." It is unclear as to what his current connection with the Litvinenko case may be.

Thallium, Polonium, or What?

Beyond those "murder" headlines, other news organizations appear to be sure about the cause of Litvinenko's death:

The *New York Times* reported "...Litvinenko died after ingesting a rare radioactive isotope, Polonium 210..." (October 14)

The *Washington Post* carried an AP story asserting that "Litvinenko died in a London hospital after ingesting a radioactive substance, polonium-210." (October 14)

But what is the reality?

While tying to find facts behind these stories, I realized that no official determination had been reported that there was a murder, or what the specific cause of death was. I contacted the coroner's office in London seeking confirmation. I wrote:

"Based on my present understanding, I will report:

"'As of now, the coroner has not determined that Litvinenko's death was a homicide. Indeed, no certification has been issued as to the cause and manner of death.'

"If that contains any inaccuracies, please correct me. Thanks."

The coroner's office responded:

"William,

"That is correct.

"Thanks for seeking clarification."

That means it's not really settled that Litvinenko's death was a homicide or that he died from polonium poisoning.

It is true that the police have pursued this as a murder, and indeed have charged Andrei Lugovoi with homicide. How can that be if the death isn't officially a murder?

Forensic psychologist Dr. Maria Tcherni explains it this way: "It often happens that police may start investigating a suspected homicide before the official determination of the cause of death is reached by the coroner. The reason is simple: a coroner may take a long time to make a decision, and the case may go cold by then. So if police have suspects in a possible homicide, they may arrest and interrogate them before there is word from the coroner."

Then What's It Called?

Where does all this leave journalists? What should Litvinenko's death have been called?

It would have been better to have called it an alleged murder. Journalists are well practiced in calling a person charged with murder as an "alleged murderer." The term "murderer" is not properly used until after there has been a conviction.

Indeed, media outlets had the good sense to use accurate designators for Lugovoi:

"Lugovoi is 'most likely poisoner'" —BBC, February 1, 2007

"...Lugovoi, charged by Britain with the murder..." —Radio Free Europe, May 31, 2007

"...Lugovoi, Britain's prime suspect..." —*St. Petersburg Times*, July 24, 2007

But even the term "alleged murder" is not

completely correct. That is because there are competing explanations for the death.

Remember the October 13, 2011 headline in the *Telegraph*, "Alexander Litvinenko may have committed suicide, says Russian suspect"?

So, the death is also an alleged suicide.

But that's still not all. Edward Jay Epstein in his March 19, 2008 *New York Sun* article suggests that Litvinenko might have been the victim of accidental contamination.

That means there are three well-publicized variants of the manner of death. There is an alleged murder, an alleged suicide, and an alleged accident.

Out of a field of three different allegations, none has been proven or ruled upon. To select any one of them is to give weight to a particular version of the story.

All in all, the correct term for the Litvinenko case should have been "suspicious death." There is no doubt about that. Use of that term does not put the journalist in the position of being an advocate for one of several competing theories. But why wasn't the term used? Why does it appear that so many journalists were rooting for one version of the story?

Journalists behaved ethically in calling Lugovoi a suspect instead of a murderer. But good judgment went out the window when it came to favoring the murder designation in advance of a coroner's verdict. What went wrong here? Where's the logic? This seems like just another flight from reality that adds to the mystery.

Why a Rebirth?

Is there a reason for the sudden reawakening of the Litvinenko story? Could this be another "managed story" effort?

The first report I saw of the reemergence was in the October 1, 2011 *New York Post*. The headline read, "Russia blamed for spy's slay." It was a short item, only 59 words. Then came the "Russia murdered Litvinenko, says top prosecutor" piece in the London *Sunday Times* for October 2. The next shoe to drop was on October 3, when the *Telegraph* ran the headline "Russia 'gave agents licence to kill' enemies of the state."

That same day coincidentally saw the opening of the Berezovsky v. Abramovich trial mentioned in Chapter 7.

In the following days, many articles appeared in various papers following the themes set out in the above stories.

On October 9, the *Sunday Express* reported that "Lawyers acting for the widow of a former Russian spy who was poisoned in London will this week demand a full inquest into his death."

An inquest was held on October 13. The coroner's office told me that the decision was made that there should be further investigation, but that the scope of it would be decided later.

However, the *London Evening Standard* quoted Litvinenko's widow, Marina Litvinenko, saying that "there will be a wide-ranging inquest into his death including an investigation into the involvement of the Russian state in his murder which is exactly what I wanted." That may be. But those details certainly were not included in the official statement released by the coroner's office.

Nevertheless, the news kept coming. By October 16, stories were proliferating of Mrs. Litvinenko soliciting donations to help pay her legal expenses. On that same day, the *Daily Mail* reported, "Mrs. Litvinenko confirmed for the first time that her husband had worked for the Security Service MI5, and Intelligence Service MI6, and that he was paid tens of thousands of pounds for his help."

Does all this sound scripted? I've seen no hard evidence that it's part of a "managed story." But there is one thing the current crop of stories has in common with the 2006 coverage: a deficit of corroborating facts.

This "rebirth" seems like *Alice in Wonderland* déjà vu.

Chapter 14
The Litvinenko Scandal

The final chapter!

MANY media reports said the Litvinenko case is a James Bond mystery. I say it's more like *Alice in Wonderland.*

In early 2007, there was an outbreak of stories announcing an impending movie about the Litvinenko poisoning to star Johnny Depp. I haven't seen anywhere that the movie was actually made. But Depp did go on to star in the 2010 Disney fantasy adventure film, *Alice in Wonderland.*

There is an inescapable irony in that.

But indeed, the media coverage of the Litvinenko case has been a fantasy adventure.

Basically what we know for sure about the Litvinenko case is that he died. We also know where he died and when he died. Beyond that, there are few corroborated details.

The Unsubstantiated Storyline

The basic media storyline is that Litvinenko was a Russian spy who became a dissident and defected to the West, turned into a sharp critic of Russian president Vladimir Putin, and was murdered in an effort to silence him.

That may be all true. But maybe it's not true. After reading a lot of news reports about this whole case, I still haven't found reliable information that supports the storyline. There are a lot of claims about the circumstances, but very few reliable facts.

One theme advanced in media reports is that Litvinenko was a "spy who knew too much." It's not even certain that he ever was a spy or that he had knowledge that led to his death. This whole version of the story just didn't hold up over time. It eventually morphed into another theme, that Litvinenko was a "thorn in the side" of Putin. There was even a statement that was dictated by Litvinenko from his deathbed that implicated Putin in the poisoning. But then it appeared that there had been some chicanery surrounding his statement, and it came out that Litvinenko didn't dictate it after all.

You can see from the media quotations presented throughout this book that the news reports simply haven't provided evidence for the theories of what happened to Litvinenko. Based on the actual facts presented, the storyline turns out to be a fantasy.

That fantasy has even been carried to a higher level in various books about this case. I've seen where authors regale readers with detailed accounts of who said what to whom along with where, when, and why. But I've got to ask how they could possibly have reliable knowledge of any of that. There are so many false stories out there that it is almost impossible to separate fact from fiction. It seems to me that the authors of those books are novelists, and that they are writing a fictionalized version of a real event.

What Went Wrong?

How did all the well-reported embellishments get around? The instant story that was told had to start somewhere. The first sign I saw was from November 11, 2006, on the KavkasCenter.com news site. This was the headline: "FSB Attempted to Murder Russian Defector in London." That seems to have set the tone for a good share of all the coverage that followed.

Where could the writers of that story have gotten such definitive information so early? Did they have inside knowledge of the plot? Or did they just make up the story to grind an ax? Why didn't journalists dig into these issues?

The phony story relied upon stereotypes that were preexistent. The tarring and feathering, and the instilling of suspicion that was perpetrated against Putin in the 1999-2001 period, set the stage for the believability of unfounded accusations. If someone had reported that it was Jimmy Carter who was behind Litvinenko's poisoning, nobody would have believed it. That would have been contrary to the image of him that's widely held. But Putin's image fit the accusation.

To an extent, the story was self-perpetuating and self-validating. Media outlets were reporting information as if it were true. But they didn't have the facts to back up their reports and didn't go beyond the assumptions others were presenting.

Sources of Influence

There was the role played later in the story by Berezovsky in promoting the "Putin did it theme." Overall, how influential was he in the coverage? In *Journalism and the Political*, Dr. Macgilchrist adds substance to the idea that he was impactful. She points out that Berezovsky is described in stories variously as "the then [1990s] powerful tycoon," "the Russian oligarch exiled in London," a "Russian multimillionaire," and "the man who was once one of the wealthiest entrepreneurs in Russia."

Macgilchrist contends, "This is a surprising turnaround for someone who in the 1990s was considered to be one of the murky powerbrokers who stripped Russia's assets in exchange for helping then President Yeltsin to maintain power."

Is the positive spin about Berezovsky in the Litvinenko stories a sign that the former had a hand in shaping those stories? And to what end?

The idea that Berezovsky might be interested in stirring up trouble for Putin is supported by Berezovsky's own words. On April 13,

2007, Bloomberg journalist Henry Meyer referred to interview comments made by Berezovsky: "I am calling for revolution and revolution is always violent." I asked Meyer who conducted that interview. He responded, "I interviewed Berezovsky." However, Berezovsky later clarified his interview statement, saying, "I do not advocate or support violence."

But, interestingly, these issues of Berezovsky's reputation and motivation didn't seem to come up much in the Litvinenko coverage. It's puzzling why they didn't. It seems he certainly had an ax to grind. Shouldn't audiences have been told that?

Instead, some outlets repeated speculation that Berezovsky himself was behind the poisoning, even though there was no apparent evidence to back up that claim.

The Victimhood Bias

Another relevant point made by Macgilchrist has to do with victimhood. She quotes an interesting blog discussion that pointed to the "repeated claims that Mr. Litvinenko was the victim of an assassination attempt by the

Kremlin."

What role did victimhood play in the Litvinenko fantasy? Dr. Tcherni explains, "It is interesting that in the current cultural climate, there is a 'sanctity-of-victim' bias. If a person is a victim of a violent crime, especially homicide or rape, it is virtually unimaginable to ask how much that person contributed to becoming a victim or to question the person's integrity or a possibly not-so-stellar past. Perhaps that's why nobody in the media really dug deeper into Litvinenko's affairs beyond the fact that he was a 'spy.'"

The "sanctity- of-victim" concept also extends to supporters of the victim. Tcherni references *Cold-Blooded Kindness* by Barbara Oakley. It expounds on how it's not only victims that receive a presumption of "good." But those who defend them are viewed as "both righteous and morally justified." What's more, Tcherni says her own research indicates that "homicide offenders and victims mostly come from the same pool of people and possess very similar characteristics in terms of demographics, background, and lifestyle. Often times it only gets decided in the last minute of an interaction or altercation who will be the victim and who will be the murderer."

These are interesting concepts to consider when trying to make sense out of the seemingly nonsensical Litvinenko story. They show there were actual benefactors of Litvinenko's victimhood. They are the defenders of the victim. They derived the perception of righteousness and moral justification from their role.

And there's still the question: victim of what?

Was Litvinenko really murdered? The media have been clear that he was. But is that just part of the fantastical story that they've palmed off as news? I've shown that this isn't a settled issue yet. The coroner has not concluded that there was a murder here, and has not specified what the actual cause of death was.

Why the Media Failed

You've seen in this book that the main story the media told about the Litvinenko case is unsubstantiated. It was indeed a phony murder story and was uncorroborated by facts.

Non-media actors such as Berezovsky and his cohorts may have played a role in shaping the story. And, Gusinsky may have played a role years ago in shaping perceptions of Putin. But they certainly have a right to their opinions and to propagate them.

Ultimately though, the responsibility for the failed coverage rests with the media. Journalism failed its audiences.

In a real sense, the media failed irrespective of whether or not their stories are ever found to be true in the end. The media failed because at the time they reported their fantastical stories, they had no valid reason to believe that they were true, based upon facts that they displayed.

Did the journalists fail to do a responsible job out of ill intent? I've seen nothing to suggest that. But why then did they neglect their responsibility?

I'll posit a few contributing factors:

First, it was easier for them to go with a

managed story that was handed to them, or to just follow the crowd in using the angle that others had taken. And it took less effort to write to their audiences' stereotypes than to explain realities that may seem counterintuitive.

Second, a simple spy story had more instant audience appeal than a complex story of intermingled relationships, hidden agendas, and unfamiliar subtleties.

Third, they lacked the expertise and resources to have done a really good job. Was this a London story, or a Russian story that just happened to play out in London? Methinks the latter. But for the most part, the news crews in charge of the story were UK based. And they were clueless about the critically important Russian subtleties of the case. Some outlets also had a Moscow correspondent. I cited one example where the Moscow journalist was of no help in straightening out the story. But another Moscow-based journalist of a UK paper told me of his fruitless efforts to correct the faulty journalism that was being committed by his colleagues in London. He said they were in control of the story and wouldn't listen to his input.

The Truth Wasn't Newsworthy

Before November 2006, Alexander Litvinenko was little known in the world. Even less was known about the work in which he was engaged. On his own merits, Litvinenko just wasn't newsworthy.

One of the most puzzling aspects of this is why the story about him grew to the proportion that it did. If Litvinenko had died in his sleep somewhere of natural causes, it would have gone virtually unnoticed in the world.

But, there were sensational claims that a Kremlin plot caused his death. Even a novice journalist should have taken care to question those as-yet-unsubstantiated allegations. But, experienced, practicing journalists didn't. They took the photos that were handed out, and ran with the story.

One irony of the case is that the odds are stacked against the truth ever coming out. In a Wikileaks-released cable from William Burns, then American ambassador in Moscow, he wrote that the Litvinenko case has "spawned a welter of conspiracy theories in Russia." He explained that the theories are "handicapped by a lack of evidence and by the existence of other motives for the killings and other potential perpetrators." And when you think of it, isn't that the case for the whole story in general. What can you really believe? Whatever the truth may ultimately be, as Burns put it in his conclusion, "...it may never be known." I think he's right about that.

But the Media's Failure is Newsworthy

In reality, the most noteworthy and newsworthy aspect of the Litvinenko case is the story itself. The tale of a phony story going viral throughout the world's established media is clearly one for the books — and should have been one for the news. But it wasn't.

Instead, the news concentrated on a nonsensical, fantasy-adventure.

There is a "Declaration of Principles on the Conduct of Journalists" that is promulgated by the International Federation of Journalists. It states:

"The journalist shall report only in

accordance with facts of which he/she knows the origin."

That didn't happen here, and the impact was of global proportion, affecting beliefs, and potentially falsely informing international policy developers. It's alarming to think how many other similarly flawed "stories" are out there and what impact they are having.

Some media outlets have been embarrassed over the years when it came out that a journalist concocted a phony story about something and presented it as factual. Those instances are nothing compared to the Litvinenko case. It's got to be the phony story of the century.

Fin

This ends the final chapter of this book on media coverage of the Litvinenko poisoning. But the final chapter of the case itself is yet to be written. Will media outlets just continue the present charade? Will movie producers really release films based on a fake premise?

They all have an opportunity to do a turnabout and choose fact-based journalism over *Alice in Wonderland*. They have a chance to do the right thing.

Which path will they choose?

Now that you know what their game has been, you can watch and make an informed judgment on what they do next.

Indeed, we'll see which path they choose!

Appendix

About the Author

William Dunkerley is a media business analyst and consultant specializing in Russia and other post-communist countries. He has written extensively for *Sreda*, Russia's first media management magazine, and for *the Moscow Times*.

Mr. Dunkerley has been a featured speaker at media business conferences in seven post-communist countries, including the World Congresses of the International Federation of Journalists and the World Association of Newspapers.

He is principal of William Dunkerley Publishing Consultants, and editor and publisher of two industry publications: *Editors Only* and the *STRAT Newsletter*.

The Russian Media Business

William Dunkerley has also authored a book about Russia's media business and its foibles. Entitled *Medvedev's Media Affairs*, particular focus is given to the role of Dmitry Medvedev who has served as Russia's president and prime minister at separate times. Information about this book is available at www.omnicompress.com/mma.

Omnicom Press

Omnicom Press, publisher of this book, was founded in 1981 to offer publishing products and printing services. It now offers print-on-demand books and e-books. The e-books can be read on PCs, laptops, notebooks, tablets, e-readers, and smartphones.

Updates

New developments are reported at:

http://www.omnicompress.com/updates-plm

For both user name and password enter:

plm9935